the metric system is

the metric system is

By Jerolyn Ann Nentl

Library of Congress Catalog Card Number: 76-24199. International Standard Book Number: 0-913940-44-5.

Design — Doris Woods and Randal M. Heise.

Special Thanks to:

Dr. Mary Kahrs - Professor of Education at Mankato
State University, Mankato, Minnesota

Mr. David L. Dye - Mathematics Consultant, St. Paul, Minnesota

PHOTO CREDITS

Mark Ahlstrom, Media House

R.M. Heise - Art Director

the metric system is

GRAM
METRIC TON
LITER
METER
KILOMETER
MILLIGRAM
MILLILITER
CELSIUS THER-MOMETER
THINK METRIC

The United States is changing to a new way of measuring things. It is a very easy system to learn. This is because it is a very orderly system with all measurements based on the number 10.

Ever since our country was founded 200 years ago, Americans have been measuring in feet and inches and yards, in pounds and ounces, in cups and pints, in quarts and gallons and in lots of other units whose names most people have a hard time remembering. Remembering what each of the units means and how to use it is even more confusing, even for adults!

The official name of the new system is Systeme International d'Unites. This is the way you say "International System of Units" if you speak the French language. The new system is usually called the **METRIC SYSTEM** in everyday conversation. The short way of writing the name is SI, meaning the "international system."

The metric system's official name is in French because it was actually developed in France almost 200 years ago. It is not a new system at all!

The Metric
System in Use

By changing from the North American system of measuring to the metric system, Americans hope to bring some order to all the confusion that has surrounded their way of measuring things for so long. Perhaps you may already be familiar with some of the units for measuring in the metric system.

If you like to take pictures with a camera, you probably already have heard of 35-millimeter still cameras, or 16-millimeter movie cameras. "Millimeter" is one of the units for measuring distance between two points in the metric system.

If you like to ski, and have bought or rented your own skis, you have heard of centimeter lengths. "Centimeter" is another unit for distance in the metric system.

If the doctor has ever given you a prescription for medicine when you were sick, it was probably measured out at the drug store in milliliters or milligrams. "Milliliter" is a unit for measuring liquids, and "milligram" is a unit for measuring mass, or weight, in the metric system.

People have been measuring things for thousands of years. They have been trying to tell each other about measurements ever since someone first asked "how far" or "how much", or "how long" or "how many", "how big" or "how hot."

We need measurements to tell each other how far it is from one town to the next, or from one country to the next or to the moon. We need them when we want to know how much milk our glass will hold, or how much gasoline a tank truck will hold. We need them when we want to know how much we weigh, or how much our truck weighs, before it goes across the bridge.

We need them when we want to know how hot to set the oven for the cake we are baking, or how cold it will get above the Arctic Circle, when explorers go there.

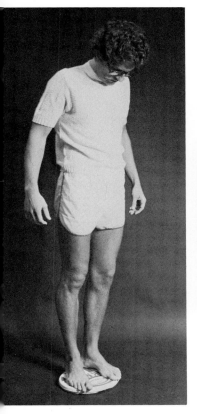

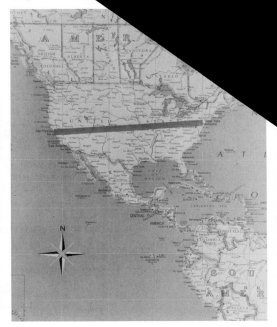

When people first started to ask and answer these questions, they used things that were the most familiar to them as their units of measurement. One of the first known measurements was the cubit.

The cubit is found in the Bible, in the story about Noah building the ark. Noah was told to build the ark "300 cubits long". People who lived in the time of Noah understood the cubit to be the distance from their fingertips to their elbow.

Other measurements were understood in relationship to other parts of people's bodies. For example: many years after Noah, King Henry I in England said that the yard was equal to the distance from the tip of his nose to the end of his thumb.

People also used things like seeds to find out how much containers would hold. They would fill a container to the top with seeds, and then empty them all out and count them.

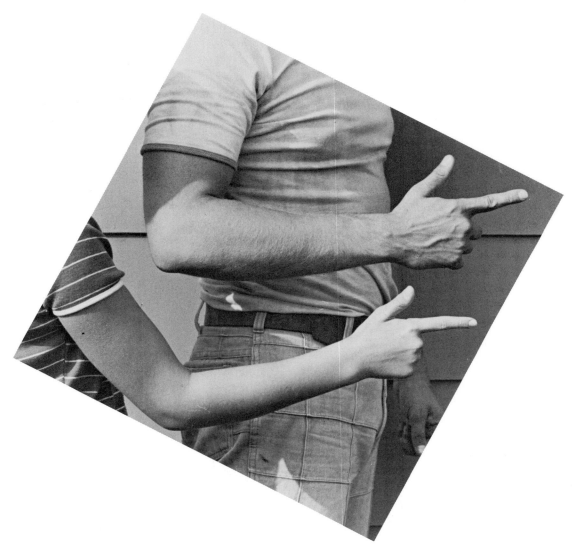

The distance from your fingertip to your elbow is not
the same distance as everyone elses.

It was very easy to make mistakes using these units of measurement. The reason is simple. The distance from your fingertips to your elbow is not the same as the distance from your father's fingertips to his elbow. Some seeds are smaller than others.

What people needed was a system for measuring things that used units that were always the same, no matter who was using them, no matter in what part of the world they were used, no matter how hot or cold it was, or how wet or dry it was.

Another way of saying this is that people needed a system that used units that were "standard".

In 1670, a Frenchman named Gabriel Mouton began telling fellow scientists and mathematicians about a system he had invented, that made measuring very easy and very accurate.

Mouton's ideas were a forerunner to the system that has come to be known as the metric system. But his ideas were not accepted very well by anybody except scientists.

America has considered changing to a system with all measurements based upon the number 10 for many years. But people were afraid of any system that was new and had strange sounding words to name its units of measurement. They resisted changing to a new system, even though the people who suggested metrics told them it would be a much easier and much better system to use.

In 1866, the United States even passed a law allowing the use of the metric system. But the law only said the people in America COULD use the metric system for all their official business. It did not say they MUST use it.

And so most Americans didn't — except the scientists.

But people in other countries were beginning to see how good the metric system was. One by one, they began to use it for all their measuring. When they traded back and forth with one another, they used the metric system to measure all their products.

But the United States still kept on using its old system.

Then, in 1957, there came a surprising and exciting announcement from Russia. Sputnik 1, the first space satellite in the history of the world, was in orbit around the earth! The announcement from Russia said that the satellite was "in orbit 900 kilometers from Earth," and that it was "58 centimeters in diameter with a mass of 83.6 kilograms."

SPUTNIK 1

Most Americans didn't know what this meant, and we still don't.

That is because they were still using the old system of measurement and so are you.

But now people wanted to know more about the metric system. They became very interested in learning how to use it.

By 1962, the metric system was in use throughout the continent of Asia, including the country of Japan. By 1965, England was also beginning to change to the metric system. America does a lot of trading with both Japan and England, and it was getting harder to understand each other when America insisted on using the old system of measurement. The approval of metrics for trade by a recent European Economic Community agreement has put even more pressure on the United States to adopt the metric system.

All but four countries in the world were using the metric system, or were in the process of changing over to it by 1976, including Canada, which is our closest neighbor.

Finally, in December of 1975, President Gerald Ford signed a law that established a U.S. Metric Board to help the country change to the metric system.

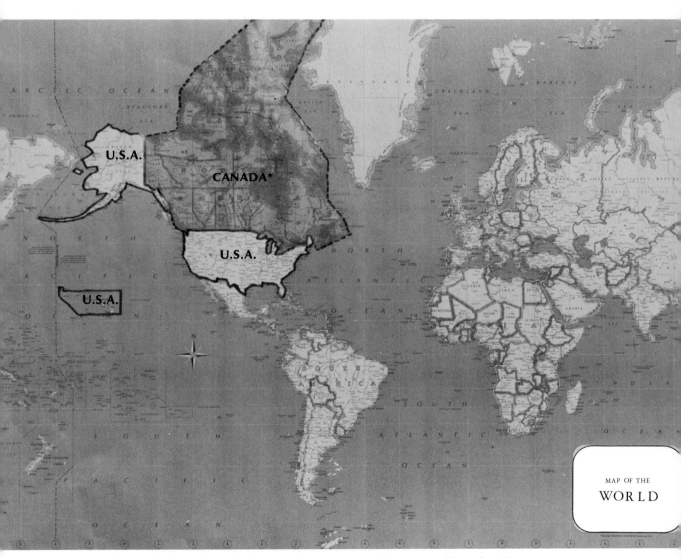

*Canada has adopted The Metric System and is now making the change over.

One of the men who worked very hard to urge America to adopt the metric system was Alexander Graham Bell, the man who invented the telephone. In 1906, he told Congress: *"All the difficulties in the metric system are in translating from one system to the other, but the moment you use the metric system alone there is no difficulty."*

The men working in Bell's laboratory had no trouble learning to use the metric system. But they did find it hard to switch back and forth from the old system to the metric system.

That is why we will no longer mention the old units of measurement in this series of books. We will learn instead to:

THINK METRIC

Then you won't have any trouble learning to use the metric system either!

Telephone
1876

ALEXANDER GRAHAM BELL

There are four basic new words to learn if you want to use the metric system:

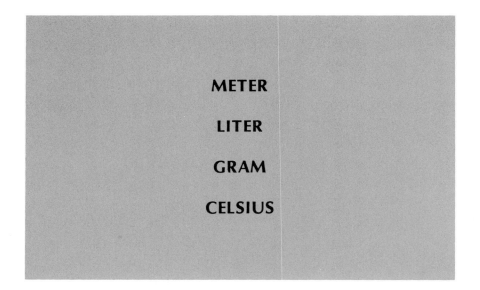

METER

LITER

GRAM

CELSIUS

Sometimes you will see meter and liter spelled "metre" and "litre". Metre and litre are the accepted SI spellings, but in many countries, including the United States, "meter" and "liter" are the common way of spelling them. You may use either spelling and be correct.

METER

is the basic unit for measuring length or distance. How long is this broom handle? How far is it to San Francisco? You can learn how to measure in meters in the book "THE METER IS" of this series.

THE LITER

is the basic unit for measuring liquid volume. How much milk is in this carton? How much gasoline does this tank truck hold? You will learn how to use the liter in the book "THE LITER IS."

KILOGRAM

is the basic unit for measuring weight or mass. How much do you weigh? How much do two nickels weigh or what is the mass of two nickels? The difference between weight and mass will be explained in the book "THE GRAM IS," and you will learn how to measure mass in grams.

DEGREE CELSIUS

is the basic unit for measuring temperature. If you are healthy, your body temperature is 37 °C. That number is read "37 degrees Celsius." You will learn all about Celsius degrees in the book "THE CELSIUS THERMOMETER IS."

There are six prefixes that can be used with the meter, the liter or the gram. Remember, a prefix is a syllable or group of syllables added to the beginning of a word.
The six prefixes are:

MILLI

CENTI

DECI

DEKA

HECTO

KILO

The first three prefixes come from the Latin language that the ancient Romans used.

MILLI means 1/1000

CENTI means 1/100

DECI means 1/10.

The other three prefixes come from the Greek language.

DEKA means 10

HECTO means 100.

KILO means 1000.

Combining these prefixes with the meter or liter or gram is easy. For example: one of the units for measuring length is CENTIMETER. It means 1/100 of a meter. Another way of saying this is: there are 100 centimeters in a meter.

Another example: one of the units for measuring weight or mass is KILOGRAM. It means 1000 grams.

Can you guess what milliliter means?

This method of using the number 10 to increase or decrease the amounts of whatever you are measuring makes arithmetic very simple. It is called a decimal system.

Why is the United States changing to the metric system?

Every important industrial country in the world except for the United States has already changed to the metric system. They use the metric system for all their trading back and forth with one another.

It is important that America be able to trade with them, too.

It will be much easier and cheaper for American manufacturers to be able to talk to each other and to manufacturers in other countries if they all talk the same measurement "language." As more and more American manufacturers begin making their products using the metric system, the American people who buy them will have to learn metrics in order to use and understand the things they buy.

Americans have always gotten used to new things very quickly! Do you or your parents or teachers remember when zip codes for letters were first announced? How about dial telephones and area codes in phone numbers? Americans resisted using these at first, but now they are able to use them very quickly and with very little effort.

But the longer we wait to completely change to metrics, the more difficult it will be to get rid of the old ways of measuring things.

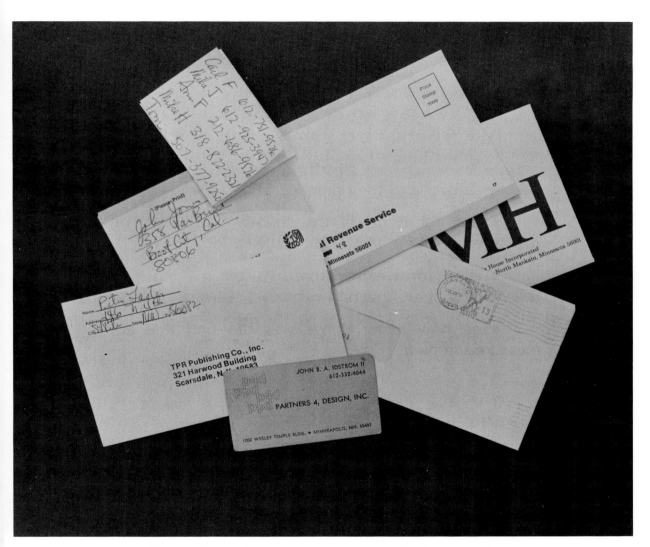

Examples of new systems now being used.

Let's THINK METRIC!

Let's learn how to use the meter, liter, gram and degree Celsius and then practice using them.

★Look for items in the grocery store that are measured in grams and liters.

★Listen for weather forecasts on the radio or television that are given in degrees Celsius.

★See how many things you can find that are measured in meters.

Remember: THINK METRIC!

LOOK FOR THE METRIC SYSTEM IN USE!

Now that you understand

the metric system

in general, learn more
about its parts.

the meter is

the liter is

the gram is

the celsius thermometer is

from